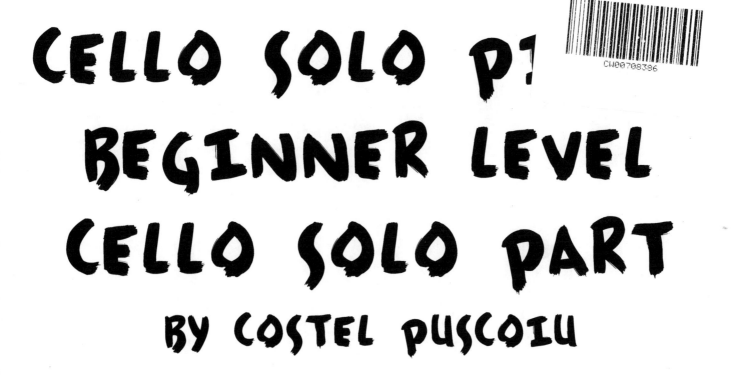

CELLO SOLO P?
BEGINNER LEVEL
CELLO SOLO PART
BY COSTEL PUSCOIU

Free piano accompaniment part download available online!
Visit: www.melbay.com/20561

BILL'S MUSIC SHELF

MB20561

Visit us on the Web at www.melbay.com or www.billsmusicshelf.com

Contents

ABOUT THE AUTHOR

Costel Puscoiu was born on August 29, 1951, in Bucharest, Romania. He studied and graduated from the Ciprian Porumbescu College of Music in Bucharest, majoring in Composition and Theory. In Romania he worked as a music teacher, and for some years he was a conductor and researcher at the Institute for Ethnology and Folklore in Bucharest. He was also a member of the Society of Romanian Composers.

His compositions comprise symphonic music (symphonies, cantatas, concertos for viola), chamber music (string quartets, sonatas for clarinet and piano, contemporary pieces for several ensembles, music for pan flute), choir pieces, and film scores. His compositions are often influenced by Romanian folklore and Byzantine liturgies. He has also contributed to several musicological and folkloristic studies and articles.

In September of 1982 Puscoiu moved to the Netherlands from his native Romania; now he is working in the Music School department as a pan flute teacher and a leader of an orchestra at the Free Academy Westvest in Delft. Meanwhile he has become a member of the Dutch Composers Association.

Spring

Allegro vivo

Costel Puscoiu
(1951)

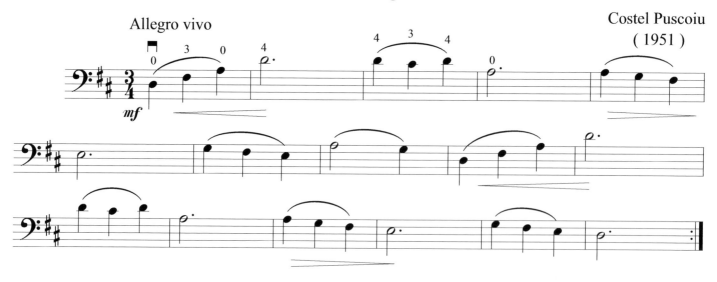

Madrigal

Andantino

Michael Praetorius
(1571 - 1621)

Hungarian Dance
(no. 1)

Allegro

Johannes Brahms
(1833 - 1897)

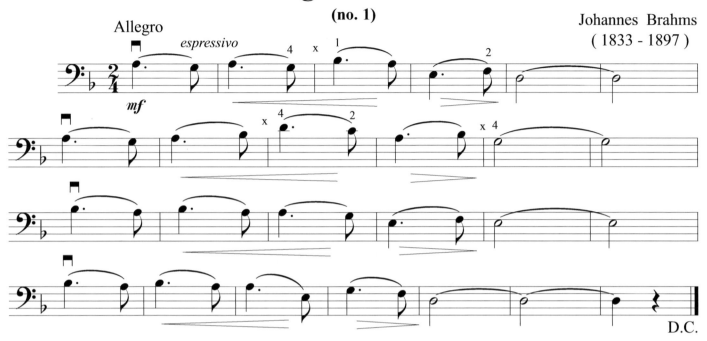

D.C.

Easy

Allegretto grazioso

Costel Puscoiu
(1951)

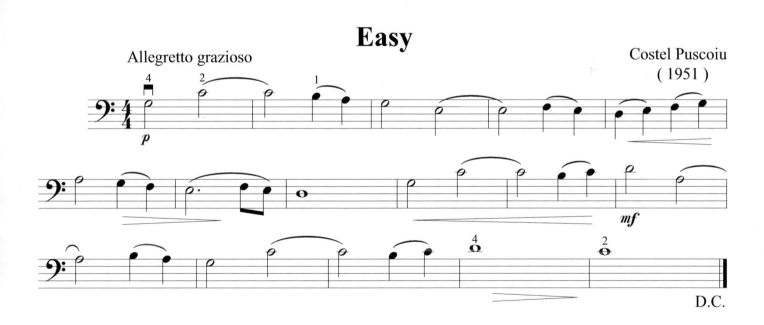

D.C.

Air
(from Sonata no. 9)

Andantino

Wolfgang Amadeus Mozart
(1756 - 1791)

March

Allegro moderato

Costel Puscoiu
(1951)

Fine

D.C. al Fine

Greensleeves

Andante

Old English Song

Melody

Tiribomba

Allegro

Italian Folk Song

D.C.

Melody

Allegretto

Nikolai Rimsky-Korsakow
(1844 - 1908)

The Beginner

Costel Puscoiu
(1951)

Moscow Nights

Allegretto

Russian Folk Song

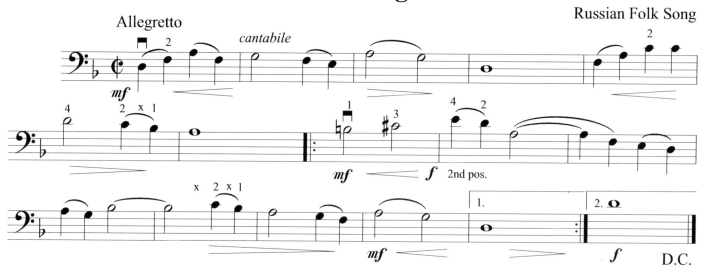

Krakowiak

Allegretto

Polish Folk Song

Pavane

Gabriel Fauré
(1845 - 1924)

Andantino cantabile

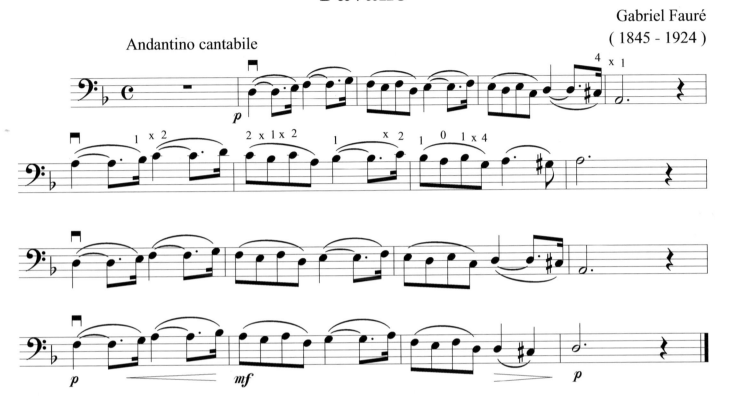

Two Pigeons

Argentinian Folk Song

Moderato

Adagio
(from Clarinet Concerto)

Wolfgang Amadeus Mozart
(1756 - 1791)

Prelude
(op. 28, no. 7)

Frédéric Chopin
(1810 - 1849)

Morning
(from "Peer Gynt")

Edvard Grieg
(1843 - 1907)

Allegretto pastorale

Album - leaf
(from "Lyric Pieces")

Edvard Grieg
(1843 - 1907)

Slavonic Dance

(op. 46, no. 2)

Romance

(op. 50)

Ludwig van Beethoven
(1770 - 1827)

Gavotte

Arcangelo Corelli
(1653 - 1713)

Papageno's Carillon
(from "The Magic Flute")

Allegretto

Wolfgang Amadeus Mozart
(1756 - 1791)

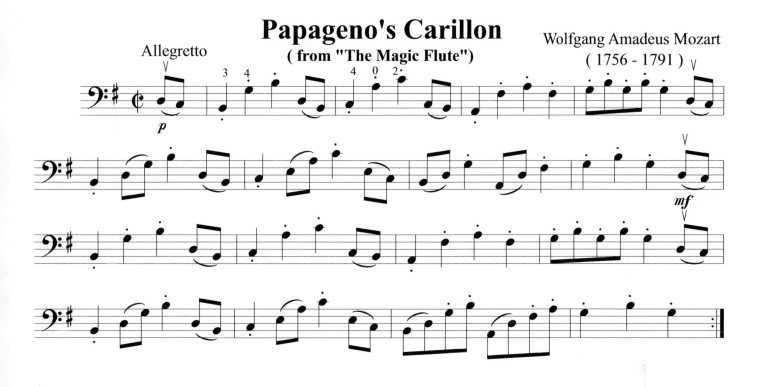

Children's Dance

Costel Puscoiu
(1951)

Made in the USA